A Note to Paren

DK READERS is a compelling program for beginning readers, designed in conjunction with leading literacy experts, including Dr. Linda Gambrell, Distinguished Professor of Education at Clemson University. Dr. Gambrell has served as President of the National Reading Conference, the College Reading Association, and the International Reading Association.

Beautiful illustrations and superb full-color photographs combine with engaging, easy-to-read stories to offer a fresh approach to each subject in the series. Each DK READER is guaranteed to capture a child's interest while developing his or her reading skills, general knowledge, and love of reading.

The five levels of DK READERS are aimed at different reading abilities, enabling you to choose the books that are exactly right for your child:

Pre-level 1: Learning to read
Level 1: Beginning to read
Level 2: Beginning to read alone
Level 3: Reading alone
Level 4: Proficient readers

The "normal" age at which a child begins to read can be anywhere from three to eight years old. Adult participation through the lower levels is very helpful for providing encouragement, discussing storylines, and sounding out unfamiliar words.

No matter which level you select, you can be sure that you are helping your child learn to read, then read to learn!

LONDON, NEW YORK, MUNICH,
MELBOURNE, and DELHI

DK LONDON
Series Editor Deborah Lock
US Senior Editor Shannon Beatty
Project Art Editor Hoa Luc
Producer, Pre-production Francesca Wardell
Illustrator Hoa Luc

Reading Consultant
Linda Gambrell, Ph.D.

DK DELHI
Editor Pomona Zaheer
Assistant Art Editor Yamini Panwar
DTP Designers Anita Yadav, Syed Md Farhan
Picture Researcher Sumedha Chopra
Deputy Managing Editor Soma B. Chowdhury

First American Edition, 2014
Published in the United States by DK Publishing
345 Hudson Street, New York, New York 10014

14 15 16 17 18 10 9 8 7 6 5 4 3
003—253411—August/14

Copyright © 2014 Dorling Kindersley Limited
All rights reserved.
Without limiting the rights under copyright reserved above,
no part of this publication may be reproduced, stored in or introduced
into a retrieval system, or transmitted, in any form, or by any means
(electronic, mechanical, photocopying, recording, or otherwise),
without the prior written permission of the copyright owner.
Published in Great Britain by Dorling Kindersley Limited.

A catalog record for this book is available
from the Library of Congress.

ISBN: 978-1-4654-2001-5 (Paperback)
ISBN: 978-1-4654-2000-8 (Hardcover)

DK books are available at special discounts when
purchased in bulk for sales promotions, premiums,
fund-raising, or educational use.
For details, contact:
DK Publishing Special Markets
345 Hudson Street, New York, New York 10014
SpecialSales@dk.com

Printed and bound in China by
South China Printing Company

The publisher would like to thank the following for
their kind permission to reproduce their photographs:
(Key: a=above, b=below/bottom, c=center, l=left, r=right, t=top)
1 Dreamstime.com: Djburrill (br). 3 Alamy Images: Zoonar/Yordan Rusev (bc).
4–29 Dreamstime.com: Djburrill (bl, br). 4 123RF.com: scusi (tl).
4–5 Dreamstime.com: Matthewennisphotography (cb). 5 Alamy Images:
Gareth Byrne (b); Dreamstime.com: Alex Ciopata (tr). 7 Alamy Images:
David J. Green – work themes. 8–9 Alamy Images: Brandon Bourdages (c).
11 Alamy Images: JG Photography (r). 12 123RF.com: scusi (tl). 13 Alamy
Images: Zoonar/Yordan Rusev. 15 Alamy Images: StockPhotosArt – Industrial;
Getty Image: George Clerk/E+ (tl) 16–17 Alamy Images: dbtravel (b).
18 123RF.com: Sabri Deniz KIZIL (tl). 19 Alamy Images: Rjh_Catalog.
20–21 Alamy Images: RJH_CATALOG. 24 123RF.com: scusi (tl).
25 Alamy Images: JoeFox/Radharc Images (b); Dreamstime.com: 3desc (cl)
26 Alamy Images: Justin Kase z02z. 27 Corbis: Ocean (b). 28 Alamy Images:
1bestofphoto (b). 28–29 Alamy Images: Zoonar/Yordan Rusev (bc). 29 Alamy
Images: Brandon Bourdages (b). 30 Dreamstime.com: 3desc (bl); Dreamstime.
com: Alex Ciopata (clb); Getty Image: George Clerk/E+ (tl).
Jacket images: Front: Dreamstime.com: Jvdwolf (b), Uatp1 (tr).

All other images © Dorling Kindersley Limited
For further information see: www.dkimages.com

Discover more at
www.dk.com

Contents

BEGINNING **1** TO READ

MEGA
Machines

Written by Deborah Lock

Stage 1
Clearing the site

"Hard hats on!"

says the foreman, getting to work.

foreman

"Welcome to
the construction site.
The plans are ready
for building a new school.
The mega machines are ready
to start work."

plans

Rumble, rumble!

"Here they come!"

This picture shows what the new school
will look like.

"What a mess!"

says the foreman,
scratching his head.
The site is not level and
it is covered with rubble.
The bulldozer, front loader,
and dump truck
are needed.
The bulldozer pushes
the dirt and rubble
with its blade.

It moves along
on crawler tracks.

Hum, rumble, hum!

The front loader scoops up the mounds of dirt and rubble.
The bucket moves.

Forward... down...

scoop...
up!

The front loader carries
its loaded bucket
raised high.

The dump truck will take
the dirt and rubble away.
The bucket of the front loader
tips up over the dumping bed.

Swish, clatter, clatter, swish!

The front loader
goes back and forth
to collect some more.

"Stage 1 is done,"

says the foreman,
nodding his head.

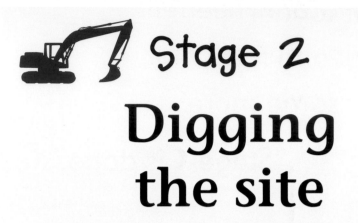

Stage 2

Digging the site

"What a noise!"

shouts the foreman, covering his ears.

The site is now clear and the excavator has arrived.

The excavator is needed
to dig some deep holes.
The arm moves.

Lower... scoop...
lift... turn...
drop...
turn!

13

Whirr, rumble, whirr!

Along comes
the concrete mixer.
The mixing drum
must keep spinning.

"Pour the concrete
into the hole,"

orders the foreman.

"Leave it
to harden."

concrete

More holes are
dug and filled.
This makes a firm base
for the new school.

15

The concrete is hard.
The holes have been filled.
Here comes the roller
to make the ground
smooth and flat.

Roll, press,
smooth!

The roller squashes down
the dirt.

"Stage 2 is done,"
says the foreman,
rubbing his ear.

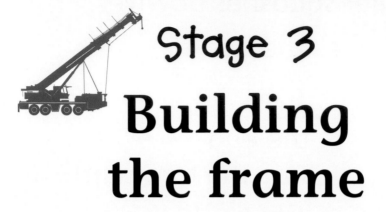

Stage 3
Building the frame

"Raise the crane,"

shouts the foreman, lifting his arms.

A large mobile crane arrives.
Up, up goes the boom.
The hook hangs from
the chain at the end
of the boom.

The long trucks bring
the strong steel girders.
The crane driver moves
the levers to lower the hook.

Lower... hook...
lift... turn...
lower... fit...
unhook!

girder

The girders are picked up
one by one on the hook.

The upright girders
are fitted together first.
The crane swings
back and forth.

Other girders
are laid across.

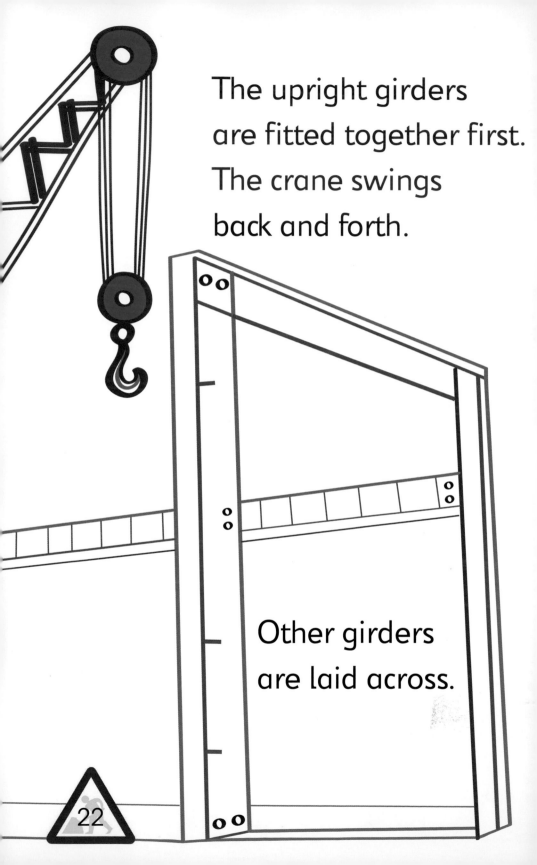

The girders will support
the floors and the roof
of the school.
The workers bolt the girders
together.

Turn, twist, hammer!

"Stage 3 is done,"

says the foreman,
wiping his forehead.

Stage 4

Finishing the school

"One month left," calls the foreman, shaking his head. The huge trucks arrive with their heavy loads.

There are concrete blocks and
white siding for the walls,
shiny windows, and tall doors.
The bricklayers spread
the mortar and lay the blocks.

siding

The workers are raised on a truck-mounted elevator.

535.95

The workers fit the siding
onto the walls.

"Two weeks left,"

shouts the foreman,
rubbing his chin.
The vans arrive.
Here are the plasterer,
the decorator, the
roofer, the plumber,
the electrician, and
the carpenter
to help.

27

"One week left.
Let's work together."

shouts the foreman,
checking the plans.
The trucks arrive with
the furniture.
Everyone helps to unload and
carry it all into the school.

"Stage 4 is done. Good job!"

says the foreman.
The new school is finished.
The mega machines
rumble away.

Rumble, hum, rumble!

Glossary

Concrete
mix of cement, sand, small stones, and water

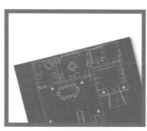

Foreman
someone who is in charge of the other workers

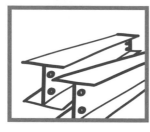

Girder
large, strong steel beam used to make the frame of a building

Plans
drawing to look like a finished building or object

Siding
layer that protects the outside of a building

Index

DK READERS help children learn to read, then read to learn. If you enjoyed this DK READER, then look out for these other titles for your child.

Level 1 Deadly Dinosaurs
Roar! Thud! Meet Rexy, Sid, Deano, and Sonia, the dinosaurs that come alive at night in the museum. Who do you think is the deadliest?

Level 1 Little Dolphin
Follow Little Dolphin's adventures when he leaves his mother and joins the older dolphins for the first time. Will he be strong enough to keep up?

Level 1 Bugs Hide and Seek
Surprise! Some bugs have the perfect shape and color to stay hidden. They look like the plants around them. Can you find them?

Level 1 Playful Puppy
Holly's dream has come true—she's been given her very own puppy. Share her delight in the playfulness of her new puppy as she tries to train him.

Level 1 Pirate Attack!
Come and join Captain Blackbeard and his pirate crew for an action-packed adventure on the high seas.